This biweekly budget planner provides a fantastic way to manage your Paychecks every two weeks. Inside , you will find a variety organized Pages that will help you to record your bills, track your expenses etc.

Belongs to : _____

Quarterly Financial Goals

First Quarter (Jan-Mar)	Second Quarter (Apr-Jun)

Third Quarter (Jul-Sep)	Fourth Quarter (Oct-Dec)

Monthly Budget

Month : _____

PAYCHECK 1

Pay Date	Expected	Actual	Notes

EXPENSES

Type	Due Date	Amount	Paid
TOTAL EXPENSES			

Monthly Budget

Month : _____

PAYCHECK 2			
Pay Date	Expected	Actual	Notes

EXPENSES			
Type	Due Date	Amount	Paid
TOTAL EXPENSES			

Extra Income Tracker

Month: _____

Source	Expected	Actual

DISTRIBUTION		
Location	Purpose	Amount
TOTAL EXTRA INCOME		

Weekly Expense Log

_____ To _____

Day	Description	Amount

Weekly Expense Log

_____ To _____

Day	Description	Amount

Notes

Notes

Quarterly Financial Goals

First Quarter (Jan-Mar)	Second Quarter (Apr-Jun)

Third Quarter (Jul-Sep)	Fourth Quarter (Oct-Dec)

Monthly Budget

Month : _____

PAYCHECK 1			
Pay Date	Expected	Actual	Notes

EXPENSES			
Type	Due Date	Amount	Paid
TOTAL EXPENSES			

Monthly Budget

Month : _____

PAYCHECK 2			
Pay Date	Expected	Actual	Notes

EXPENSES			
Type	Due Date	Amount	Paid
TOTAL EXPENSES			

Extra Income Tracker

Month: _____

Source	Expected	Actual

DISTRIBUTION		
Location	Purpose	Amount
TOTAL EXTRA INCOME		

Weekly Expense Log

_____ To _____

Day	Description	Amount

Weekly Expense Log

_____ To _____

Day	Description	Amount

Notes

Notes

Quarterly Financial Goals

First Quarter (Jan-Mar)	Second Quarter (Apr-Jun)

Third Quarter (Jul-Sep)	Fourth Quarter (Oct-Dec)

Monthly Budget

Month : _____

PAYCHECK 1

Pay Date	Expected	Actual	Notes

EXPENSES

Type	Due Date	Amount	Paid
TOTAL EXPENSES			

Monthly Budget

Month: _____

PAYCHECK 2			
Pay Date	Expected	Actual	Notes

EXPENSES			
Type	Due Date	Amount	Paid
TOTAL EXPENSES			

Extra Income Tracker

Month: _____

Source	Expected	Actual

DISTRIBUTION

Location	Purpose	Amount
TOTAL EXTRA INCOME		

Weekly Expense Log

_____ To _____

Day	Description	Amount

Weekly Expense Log

_____ To _____

Day	Description	Amount

Notes

Notes

Quarterly Financial Goals

First Quarter (Jan-Mar)	Second Quarter (Apr-Jun)

Third Quarter (Jul-Sep)	Fourth Quarter (Oct-Dec)

Monthly Budget

Month: _____

PAYCHECK 1			
Pay Date	Expected	Actual	Notes

EXPENSES			
Type	Due Date	Amount	Paid
TOTAL EXPENSES			

Monthly Budget

Month : _____

PAYCHECK 2			
Pay Date	Expected	Actual	Notes

EXPENSES			
Type	Due Date	Amount	Paid
TOTAL EXPENSES			

Extra Income Tracker

Month: _____

Source	Expected	Actual

DISTRIBUTION

Location	Purpose	Amount
TOTAL EXTRA INCOME		

Weekly Expense Log

_____ To _____

Day	Description	Amount

Weekly Expense Log

_____ To _____

Day	Description	Amount

Notes

Notes

Quarterly Financial Goals

First Quarter (Jan-Mar)	Second Quarter (Apr-Jun)

Third Quarter (Jul-Sep)	Fourth Quarter (Oct-Dec)

Monthly Budget

Month : _____

PAYCHECK 1			
Pay Date	Expected	Actual	Notes

EXPENSES			
Type	Due Date	Amount	Paid
TOTAL EXPENSES			

Monthly Budget

Month : _____

PAYCHECK 2			
Pay Date	Expected	Actual	Notes

EXPENSES			
Type	Due Date	Amount	Paid
TOTAL EXPENSES			

Extra Income Tracker

Month : _____

Source	Expected	Actual

DISTRIBUTION

Location	Purpose	Amount
TOTAL EXTRA INCOME		

Weekly Expense Log

_____ To _____

Day	Description	Amount

Weekly Expense Log

_____ To _____

Day	Description	Amount

Notes

Notes

Quarterly Financial Goals

First Quarter (Jan-Mar)	Second Quarter (Apr-Jun)

Third Quarter (Jul-Sep)	Fourth Quarter (Oct-Dec)

Monthly Budget

Month : _____

PAYCHECK 1

Pay Date	Expected	Actual	Notes

EXPENSES

Type	Due Date	Amount	Paid
TOTAL EXPENSES			

Monthly Budget

Month : _____

PAYCHECK 2

Pay Date	Expected	Actual	Notes

EXPENSES

Type	Due Date	Amount	Paid
TOTAL EXPENSES			

Extra Income Tracker

Month: _____

Source	Expected	Actual

DISTRIBUTION

Location	Purpose	Amount
TOTAL EXTRA INCOME		

Weekly Expense Log

_____ To _____

Day	Description	Amount

Weekly Expense Log

_____ To _____

Day	Description	Amount

Notes

Notes

Quarterly Financial Goals

First Quarter (Jan-Mar)	Second Quarter (Apr-Jun)
Third Quarter (Jul-Sep)	**Fourth Quarter (Oct-Dec)**

Monthly Budget

Month : _____

PAYCHECK 1

Pay Date	Expected	Actual	Notes

EXPENSES

Type	Due Date	Amount	Paid
TOTAL EXPENSES			

Monthly Budget

Month : _____

PAYCHECK 2			
Pay Date	Expected	Actual	Notes

EXPENSES			
Type	Due Date	Amount	Paid
TOTAL EXPENSES			

Extra Income Tracker

Month: _____

Source	Expected	Actual

DISTRIBUTION

Location	Purpose	Amount
TOTAL EXTRA INCOME		

Weekly Expense Log

_____ To _____

Day	Description	Amount

Weekly Expense Log

_____ To _____

Day	Description	Amount

Notes

Notes

Quarterly Financial Goals

First Quarter (Jan-Mar)	Second Quarter (Apr-Jun)

Third Quarter (Jul-Sep)	Fourth Quarter (Oct-Dec)

Monthly Budget

Month : _____

PAYCHECK 1

Pay Date	Expected	Actual	Notes

EXPENSES

Type	Due Date	Amount	Paid
TOTAL EXPENSES			

Monthly Budget

Month : _____

PAYCHECK 2			
Pay Date	Expected	Actual	Notes

EXPENSES			
Type	Due Date	Amount	Paid
TOTAL EXPENSES			

xtra Income Tracker

Month: _____

Source	Expected	Actual

DISTRIBUTION		
Location	Purpose	Amount
TOTAL EXTRA INCOME		

Weekly Expense Log

_____ To _____

Day	Description	Amount

Weekly Expense Log

_____ To _____

Day	Description	Amount

Notes

Notes

Quarterly Financial Goals

First Quarter (Jan-Mar)	Second Quarter (Apr-Jun)
Third Quarter (Jul-Sep)	Fourth Quarter (Oct-Dec)

Monthly Budget

PAYCHECK 1

Pay Date	Expected	Actual	Notes

EXPENSES

Type	Due Date	Amount	Paid
TOTAL EXPENSES			

Monthly Budget

Month : _____

PAYCHECK 2			
Pay Date	Expected	Actual	Notes

EXPENSES			
Type	Due Date	Amount	Paid
TOTAL EXPENSES			

xtra Income Tracker

Month : _____

Source	Expected	Actual

DISTRIBUTION		
Location	Purpose	Amount
TOTAL EXTRA INCOME		

Weekly Expense Log

_____ To _____

Day	Description	Amount

Weekly Expense Log

_____ To _____

Day	Description	Amount

Notes

Notes

Quarterly Financial Goals

First Quarter (Jan-Mar)	Second Quarter (Apr-Jun)
Third Quarter (Jul-Sep)	Fourth Quarter (Oct-Dec)

Monthly Budget

Month : _____

PAYCHECK 1

Pay Date	Expected	Actual	Notes

EXPENSES

Type	Due Date	Amount	Paid
TOTAL EXPENSES			

Monthly Budget

Month : _____

PAYCHECK 2			
Pay Date	Expected	Actual	Notes

EXPENSES			
Type	Due Date	Amount	Paid
TOTAL EXPENSES			

xtra Income Tracker

Month: _____

Source	Expected	Actual

DISTRIBUTION		
Location	Purpose	Amount
TOTAL EXTRA INCOME		

Weekly Expense Log

_____ To _____

Day	Description	Amount

Weekly Expense Log _____ To _____

Day	Description	Amount

Notes

Notes

Quarterly Financial Goals

First Quarter (Jan-Mar)	Second Quarter (Apr-Jun)

Third Quarter (Jul-Sep)	Fourth Quarter (Oct-Dec)

Monthly Budget

Month : _____

PAYCHECK 1			
Pay Date	Expected	Actual	Notes

EXPENSES			
Type	Due Date	Amount	Paid
TOTAL EXPENSES			

Monthly Budget

Month : _____

PAYCHECK 2			
Pay Date	Expected	Actual	Notes

EXPENSES			
Type	Due Date	Amount	Paid
TOTAL EXPENSES			

xtra Income Tracker

Month : _____

Source	Expected	Actual

DISTRIBUTION

Location	Purpose	Amount
TOTAL EXTRA INCOME		

Weekly Expense Log

_____ To _____

Day	Description	Amount

Weekly Expense Log

_____ To _____

Day	Description	Amount

Notes

Notes

Quarterly Financial Goals

First Quarter (Jan-Mar)	Second Quarter (Apr-Jun)
Third Quarter (Jul-Sep)	Fourth Quarter (Oct-Dec)

Monthly Budget

Month : _____

PAYCHECK 1

Pay Date	Expected	Actual	Notes

EXPENSES

Type	Due Date	Amount	Paid
TOTAL EXPENSES			

Monthly Budget

Month : _____

PAYCHECK 2

Pay Date	Expected	Actual	Notes

EXPENSES

Type	Due Date	Amount	Paid
TOTAL EXPENSES			

xtra Income Tracker

Month : _____

Source	Expected	Actual

DISTRIBUTION		
Location	Purpose	Amount
TOTAL EXTRA INCOME		

Weekly Expense Log

_____ To _____

Day	Description	Amount

Weekly Expense Log

_____ To _____

Day	Description	Amount

Notes

Notes

Quarterly Financial Goals

First Quarter (Jan-Mar)	Second Quarter (Apr-Jun)
Third Quarter (Jul-Sep)	**Fourth Quarter (Oct-Dec)**

Monthly Budget

Month: _____

PAYCHECK 1			
Pay Date	Expected	Actual	Notes

EXPENSES			
Type	Due Date	Amount	Paid
TOTAL EXPENSES			

Monthly Budget

Month : _____

PAYCHECK 2			
Pay Date	Expected	Actual	Notes

EXPENSES			
Type	Due Date	Amount	Paid
TOTAL EXPENSES			

xtra Income Tracker

Month: _____

Source	Expected	Actual

DISTRIBUTION

Location	Purpose	Amount
TOTAL EXTRA INCOME		

Weekly Expense Log

_____ To _____

Day	Description	Amount

Weekly Expense Log

_____ To _____

Day	Description	Amount

Notes

Notes

Made in the USA
Las Vegas, NV
29 August 2023